The Chainlink Fence

Little Girl Photo

The studio portrait of me at age three or four is in my study at home in California. I am in a beautiful crimson challis dress, holding the skirt as if I am about to curtsy.

"How's this?" I smile and ask. The two men, Father and the photographer Mr. Yudkoff, are together peering inside a narrow black box on long legs that is draped with black cloth. They smile back at me. There is a click and flash of light.

In the portrait, my eyes do not show that my parents quarreled that morning. I know that is why my father, alone, took me to the studio. I remember his preoccupied expression when I glanced at his eyes for reassurance. I remember how his hand felt holding mine as we walked from the subway to the studio.

The Chainlink Fence

A West Coast Woman's Memories of Her East Coast Beginnings

NAOMI LAVORI

The Chain Link Fence
Copyright © 2015 by Naomi Lavori

All rights reserved. No part of this book may be reproduced in any form or by any electronic or mechanical means including information storage and retrieval systems, without permission in writing from the author. The only exception is by a reviewer, who may quote short excerpts in a review.

ISBN 978-1-935914-56-3

Cover and interior design by River Sanctuary Graphic Arts

Printed in the United States of America

To order additional copies please visit:
www.riversanctuarypublishing.com

Library of Congress Catalog Number: 2015936933

River Sanctuary Publishing
P.O Box 1561
Felton, CA 95018
www.riversanctuarypublishing.com

Dedicated to the awakening of the New Earth

> Those who have known an impassioned childhood will understand this dread of utterance about any shame connected with their parents or about their family life in any way.
>
> —George Eliot, *Daniel Deronda*

> Unto thee, let thine own times as an old story be.
>
> —John Donne

> A chain link fence is a boundary you cannot pass through, but you can see through.
>
> You can see but cannot touch. You can approach but only so far. Is someone kept in or is someone kept out?
>
> After this question is answered, the challenge becomes acceptance.
>
> —Naomi Lavori

Contents

Prologue

Chapter 1: Sea Gate …The Chainlink Fence...................... 1

Chapter 2: Sea Gate … Injustice 3

Chapter 3: Washington Heights … Terrors 4

Chapter 4: Coney Island … Candy Store........................... 5

Chapter 5: Sea Gate … Playing Hooky............................... 7

Chapter 6: Manhattan Friends … Furs 10

Chapter 7: Sea Gate … Tannhauser and Aida 12

Chapter 8: Sea Gate … P.S. 188 and Beach 44th Street...15

Chapter 9: Junior High School … Escape or Banishment..........18

Chapter 10: Florida… Miami Beach High School....................... 22

Chapter 11: Sea Gate and Sheepshead Bay … Daddy, the Crush, and the Business of Forgetting 24

Chapter 12: Sheepshead Bay… Brooklyn College 29

Chapter 13: Brighton Beach … "Sadie, Sadie, Married Lady" 34

Chapter 14: Lincoln, Massachusetts … Nana Mary 37

Chapter 15: Brighton Beach … Abandoned Accounts..............39

Chapter 16: Brighton Beach … Cards and Notes 42

Chapter 17: Brighton Beach ... On the 14th Floor............................ 46

Chapter 18: Coney Island Avenue ... Nursing Home..................... 51

Chapter 19: Coney Island Nursing Home ... Entertainment and Straw Hats.. 56

Chapter 20: Coney Island Nursing Home ... Balloons................. 59

Chapter 21: Coney Island Nursing Home ... Night Visit 62

Chapter 22: Manhattan: 86th and Broadway ... The Subway... 64

Chapter 23: Coney Island Nursing Home ... New York Times 66

Chapter 24: Brooklyn and Manhattan ... Swan Lake.................... 68

Chapter 25: Boston and Palo Alto... "Mess It Up"......................... 71

Epilogue: The Hole in the Chainlink Fence (poem)...................... 74

Acknowledgments

Prologue

There is, among the collection of framed photos in my study in California, a black and white snapshot of my parents before they were married. Their fingertips touch delicately on her lap as they sit close together on the metal railing in a park somewhere in New York, perhaps in Central Park or Prospect Park in Brooklyn. They look young and happy. Mother is wearing a beautiful long white fur stole—no doubt fashionable then—over an elegant dark costume. Father looks handsome, slender, and continental in a dark suit and tie. There is a mood of Sunday best and celebration. I seem to know the fur was a gift from her father, my grandfather. The pictured couple both seem proud of her glamorous appearance. They are attractive and clearly in love. Every time I notice this photograph in its small elegant carved frame, I have the sensation of a blow to my forehead.

From my vantage point years later, I know what this beautiful couple did not know: they will be wretchedly unhappy with each other. Mother's actions and responses to life will twist, and Father's sense of responsibility will prevent his abandoning her no matter what the provocation. This locks them both in a life-long struggle from which neither escape.

Chapter 1

Sea Gate

The Chainlink Fence

The opening in the chainlink fence near the railroad tracks is exactly big enough to crawl through. Wooden trolley tracks in the wide open fields invite walking. A thrill of pleasure from the sunny summer warmth and the wild grass and flowering weeds between the tracks and the happiness of privacy and the great freedom propel me easily down the ladder-like path. For some mysterious reason I am living with strangers. There are other little children in the household, so playing makes each long day heady with intense emotion… but now there is joyous isolation, solitary freedom.

My mother was behind another chainlink fence across the street from the house where some other woman was bathing and feeding me. I know now she was recuperating but I do not know from what. I remember once being taken by my father so she and I could see each other through the metal fence and I cried with deepest grief and longing at our separation. In my memory, she looks beautiful. A darkly flowered robe showed her beautiful figure; her black hair was pulled back in what must have been a chignon. She stood in the shadows among the flowering hedges behind the chainlink fence.

Maybe she cried too. The yearning ended abruptly, I am sure, when I was back playing with the other children.

When I am ready to retrace my steps, it seems an easy and sure thing to turn and go back on the old splintered wooden railroad ties. Somehow reversing direction is not enough because, terrifyingly, the little opening is gone. I cannot find my way back to safety, food, and familiarity. I keep searching, going back and forth from the edge of the tracks to edges of property that backed onto the abandoned tracks and empty fields. The sun that seemed glorious is now making me too hot, and the pleasant buzzing and humming now make me dizzy and itchy. I become tired and scared.

Somehow, after a while the opening is found, much further along than it should have been. Angry and agitated adults are in the backyard; I was gone long enough to have been missed. I was scolded. I was spanked. I napped. I had become tired from stumbling, searching, and fright.

Those early sensations of walking on wooden railroad tracks have just come back now, over fifty years later, whenever I shortcut across Caltrain tracks and walk a few paces on the wooden ties to get to work. The sensation of solitude of being out in the wide world alone returns, and I feel tenderness for the little girl. A sad stillness arises inside me even now that I cannot relieve her terror at being lost. It is as if she is still looking for the opening that has mysteriously disappeared and she cannot find her way back to a safe haven.

Chapter 2

Sea Gate

Injustice

Playing was life that summer. A moment was too much to lose. The little boys did not have to go into the house when Nature called. They stood on the curb and made small watery arcs into the street. Having to leave the bliss of sidewalk games with the others was a lost, precious experience. One day, determined to share in this privilege, I decided I would do what they did and not miss any playing. I put my hands where they put theirs and attempted to make an arc but just got my fingers, legs, and socks wet. I was spanked and scolded; I was consumed with a furious sense of injustice at the punishment: all I wanted was to do the same as the boys.

Now grown up, when I visit Paris, I see evidence of that gift of creating such watery arcs still manifest on exterior courtyard walls and along the boulevards.

Chapter 3

Washington Heights
Terrors

Mysterious silent slow moving lights slide on the ceiling over the crib. I do not know they are lights of passing cars.

Feeling frightened in my crib in my parents' bedroom, I want to put the fright onto something I can imagine. I know the word ghost from my playmates. I know it means something scary. I conjure up an image of a ghost. It would be an adult-sized black bird standing upright on two legs with large, long feathered wings. The wings are the length of its whole side and it has a small sharp yellow beak. *That* must be a ghost!

Over 60 years have passed, and yet I remember dreaming in my crib that I was standing very close to that bird, I was with it, it had its black feathered wing around me, it had me in its thrall. It had *me*; I was powerless to escape. There was fear in my belly. In my adult life, I came across a description of just such a figure of terror: a classic demon in human consciousness. Does the image derive from earliest racial memory? From our vulnerability to flying creatures as we took our first steps out of water onto dry land?

Chapter 4

Coney Island
Candy Store

I am very small
I hold Mother's hand
We stand together amidst vibrant street life
On an avenue, Mermaid or Neptune
In Coney Island

Summertime smells
Golden light
Luminous blue sky

No supermarkets
Comfortable old awnings shade the shops
Fruit and bakeries
White tiles and sawdust cover butcher's floor
Mystery

Rich cream tops the Charlotte Russe
Outside the candy store
Under the glass display
Like precious artifacts in museums
Forbidden fragrance from within
Treasure cave

Chocolate syrup, ice cream sodas
Vanilla mello-rolls
All manner of creamy delight

Shiny colored comic books with super hero covers
Glisten, gleam, twinkle
Give off giddy-making fragrance

Shazam!
Captain Marvel!
Batman!
Wonder Woman!
Oh rapture! Oh delight!

Backward, turn backward, O time in thy flight.
Make me a child again, just for tonight.

In *Rock Me to Sleep* by Elizabeth Chase Allen

Chapter 5

Sea Gate
Playing Hooky

We are great friends, confidantes, intimates with secrets kept just between us and hidden from my father. I am 10 or 11 years old when she shares her secrets. She has "friends" two in particular whose existence my father should not know about. She justifies this in the case she builds to me against my father. If the phone rings and my father answers, someone hangs up. I know who the someone is. We are like sisters, folks would say. Much laughter and winking and heart-to-hearts, but under it all I feel an uneasiness. I don't know why. I am "lucky," I think. Yet I envy my friends.

Their home lives seem normal; their surroundings are civilized. Routines exist in their households and in their lives. Their mothers dress them in conventional ways, not in random theatrical combinations. I daydream about pretty dresses. I go to sleep at night making up pretend pretty blouses. One would have tiny red and white checks with a round collar and little puff sleeves. The puff sleeves seem thrilling. The bright moon shines directly on me in the double bed I sleep in with my mother. I see other girls in nice raincoats carrying pretty pocketbooks. I think of how I will dress a daughter if ever I have one.

One time I am told on the last school day before Easter vacation that after the holiday, I may be put back in first grade if my continual late morning arrivals do not change. I feel frightened and disgraced. When I tell Mother, she agrees that we should not tell Father. "We'll keep it a secret." I feel relieved and, again, lucky that she is protecting me, but I still feel awfully disgraced and shamed.

It was not unusual to come home from school and find her cooking hamburgers to wrap up, and for us to then run to the Surf Theater and see a movie, right in the middle of the week! It was necessary to get there before 5 o'clock when the prices changed from matinee to evening rates. I usually had to run ahead to get there seconds before 5 to purchase the tickets. Once the ticket seller glared and scolded me, "You always do this." We would sit in the balcony and eat our delicious food and watch a movie together, getting home before my father returned from work. After supper, he did the dishes.

Often, with an air of adventure, she asks if I would like to skip school, and we go downtown to Union Square to May's or S. Klein's where we might buy something. Or we might go to De Kalb Avenue and Abraham & Strauss to "just look," for the fun of it, without ever buying anything. At the end of De Kalb Avenue there is a Paramount movie theater and, above it, a Chinese restaurant. A feeling of secrecy and stolen pleasure accompanies a meal followed by a movie. We are two girlfriends playing hooky from conventional life. She likes the image of herself as a gypsy. The moon is low in the winter sky over the ocean when we walk in the cold from the bus to the apartment.

These outings, during my elementary school years, cultivated in me a superficial belief that I was fortunate to have this special relationship with my mother. Not until I was a mother myself did it become apparent to me how inappropriate, damaging, and destructive for both of us was this false friendship. If nothing else, it undermined my academic achievement: I formed no study habits. I did well in anything for which I had innate ability, but for any subject that required application, I did not know how to summon that ability or even to think it worthwhile to learn how. The pattern was set. Responsibility was something one could choose to avoid.

Chapter 6

Manhattan Friends

Furs

Stefano and Divani were furriers and "gayboy" friends of my mother. Of course those were not their real names. They had fancied them up. She met them through her friend Wally. We visit their Manhattan workshop on a sweltering July day during my junior high summer vacation. The city steams, buzzes, and bubbles from the heat, so the dark workshop seems a refuge.

Shadowy, slanting daylight from the alley between the office building next door and nearby warehouses lit large flat work tables. There were high ceilings, mysterious machines, and every kind of thread and needle. I try sewing a fur pom-pom on a thick lace, "to help." They would have to undo my stitches after we left.

Stefano's young amour was lounging about. "I can't do anything with him," Stefano murmured, theatrically rolling his eyes and sighing after the slender, fair boy left the loft. "All day long he just lies on the couch and smokes." Stefano's belly moved along with his shoulders as he shrugged them in delicious mock despair. We nodded in sympathy with his disapproval, although I was thrilled with the decadence of it.

Two very skinny giggly, high heeled secretaries from a nearby office came in to see "the boys" while we were there. They had on lots of lipstick and jumped about laughing and talking, visibly excited. But by what? I felt their excitement but couldn't get the source of it, especially since I "knew" about Stefano and Divani. Why would the young women be so fluttery-silly and skittish?

"You look like you come from the beach," one of them said to my mother, disparagingly, I thought. "I do," mother said, shrugging and indifferent to the implied criticism. She reached up to adjust her black hair, rolled in a loose pompadour. In contrast to the girdled, stockinged, sharp, slick suits, and glamorous make-up of the young women, mother was wearing a white open-weave, cap-sleeved dress, showing her bare arms. Very "summer time!" The most beach-like item was the woven huaraches on her feet, as well as her bare legs. I felt somehow embarrassed that she was not as rigged out as the two young women.

I thought *they* looked great.

Chapter 7

Sea Gate

Tannhauser and Aida

Mother's close and only friend before Wally, her "gayboy" friend was Faye Posner. Faye lived just inside the gate of Sea Gate with her mother and two sisters, I believe. She died before the friendship with Wally. Faye had the prettiest face and cleverest mind. Brilliant, really. She was always beautifully dressed. My recollection of her in my mother's life precedes my going to kindergarten. We were close in height because Faye was physically handicapped. She had an abnormal prominence on her back and she was not adult-sized. Standing behind her in a doorway once, I ran my small hand slowly over the bump to feel it. She turned, surprised, possibly angry, but smiled kindly at me. We said nothing.

It seemed a pleasant household of women. The senior Mrs. P., Faye's mother, was minding me one day and served me a nice little lunch. She squeezed the baked potato on my plate to break the skin and put fragrant butter on top to melt. It smelled wonderful, and my mouth wanted to eat it, but I refused. Her hands were covered with wrinkles that repulsed me; I thought they would get on the potato and somehow in or on me. When she asked why I wouldn't eat it, I shook my head and said nothing.

There was "at-home type work" in their house. No doubt low-paid work that homebound persons could do. I "helped" once, connecting small pieces of leather through each other, forming belts. Once Mother was showing Faye a matching coat and hat for me. It was a red and green plaid wool with a green velvet collar and a green ribbon on the hat that tied under my chin. I heard her say she would bring it back to the store. Although I was barely four years old, I knew to pull off the price tag and the splendid outfit would be mine!

One afternoon, Mother tells me, she and Faye went to hear Tannhauser, sat in the balcony, and got the giggles to such a degree when the opera singer sang that they left, forfeiting the performance. I can see them in my mind's eye so clearly, getting hysterics, and I can visualize the performer with her brass shield and blond braids doing her Wagnerian thing. Once you would start to "lose it," how could you stop? How not to laugh?

No one I knew had a mother with friends or stories like that. As an adult, I encountered a woman with the physical attributes that reminded me of Faye. I set about to make her my friend and I did.

Once I went to the opera to see and hear Aida. My first, an important occasion, and all important persons were present: Mother, Father, Grampa, Faye, and my grade school self. An official roll call would have found all adults from early childhood memory present and accounted for.

The curtain drops on the final scene. Applause cascades forward. The final notes from the tomb of Hashverus and Aida's "Farewell to the Earth" hang in the air. It was too much. I burst into deep, heartfelt, shuddering, aching sobs.

"She's not really dead."

"He's not really dead."

"It's only a story."

"They're not really dead."

Comforting, smiling, reassuring faces lean toward me: Grampa, Father, Faye. I do not remember Mother's face or words added to the comfort chorus. She, no doubt, would have known that I knew "they weren't really dead."

"How stupid they are. How stupid they are," I think. Of course, she's not really dead. I know that! What difference does *that* make? Don't they see how sad, how tragic, how awful it is that they died for love, even though it's only a story.

Oh the power, the rapture, the tragic force of love!

Chapter 8

Sea Gate

P.S. 188 and Beach 44th Street

I grow up where open sky, ocean, rocks, jetties, lagoons, sea gulls, and sandy beaches offer powerful assurances that the world is beautiful. Its sheer expanse also cues me that escape is possible. Meanwhile, I have a secret love. I am allowed to take the trolley to the last stop before you transfer to the subway for "The City" at Stillwell Avenue. Under the elevated subway tracks is the Library. Here, I am happy. Here exists all that is precious, desirable, and missing from my actual life: quiet, peace, and orderliness. Everything is catalogued; voices are modulated. Library bindings on books with the thick, yellowish pages still fill me with pleasure. If a librarian has inked letters and numbers in white on the spine, I smile with fond happiness. My image of Heaven, if it exists, is the Library on Stillwell Avenue.

It is second grade when penmanship is taught. We have wooden holders, which fit in your hand just right, and silver-colored metal pen points. They are distributed in a silent, attentive classroom. This is serious stuff. A rite of passage, for sure. You inserted the stub into the wooden holder and practice dipping the point in real ink and writing without getting a blot on the yellow lined paper. When Mother accompanies me to the library for the official event (getting my library card), there is silence as the librarian and Mother watch me write my name in real writing (not printing) with a pen that must be dipped in ink. A blot will not do. I remember exactly the effort of mental concentration and physical coordination. Something serious and important is happening here. The two adult women watch me without speaking to me or each other; small talk would be inappropriate to the occasion. I receive my passport to power and pleasure! The first book I sign-out that very day with my new library card is *How the Leopard Got His Spots*. What a triumph flows through me. It is nice that Mother makes a State Occasion of it. She has gotten all dressed up.

It is all changed and gone now. While in Brooklyn, to put Mother in the nursing home, my daughter drives me to the old neighborhood. I want her to see how beautiful it was where I grew up and to not have her image of Brooklyn be the one where we are together carrying out the necessary but wrenching task at hand.

The early morning sun shines. The parachute jump and the roller coaster, closed for the winter, stand like skeletal structures. Nathan's Hot Dogs is boarded. High buildings alter completely the beach front; the small neighborhood feeling is gone. I glance toward the area where the library should be, but changes have made it all unfamiliar. We drive on and pass the gate that separates

Coney Island from where I grew up in Sea Gate. A bit of luck is that a member of the family that owned the house is still there, at home, and welcoming after forty years. I am able to show the attic apartment, now totally civilized in appearance, to my daughter. I am stunned with the impact: excited and barely able to speak. How curious that the view through the window shows the ocean just where it was all that long time ago.

Chapter 9

Junior High School
Escape or Banishment

My mother, having taken it upon herself, sends me away for my "health." I am at Grand Central Station on a train called "The Silver Meteor" about to leave my home, schoolmates, and daily contact with my father. A telegram has been sent to my grandfather in Florida to meet the train. Neither my grandfather nor my father were consulted; neither participated in her decisions or actions. My father will come home from work that night and be informed. I cannot imagine what must have transpired between them; how great must have been her desire and her drive to have me elsewhere. *She* is not alone. *She* is in the company of Wally. He is the young homosexual with whom she spends most of her time. They are continuously laughing at private jokes and secrets and making plans. I *had* been frequently included in their outings and ramblings around the city. Another secret.

As the train pulls out of the station, I stand by my seat solemnly looking out the window at her. She runs on the platform alongside the train as long as possible, waving good-bye with her beautiful smile, tears streaming down her face. She is wearing a light blue Chesterfield coat over navy slacks and a matching navy and light blue tweed pattern wool scarf, wound around her head to look like a chic turban.

This event in the middle of seventh grade establishes a pattern that was not to change. I spend the school years through high school with my grandfather and summers with Mother and Father. My grandfather's retirement years and peaceful established bachelor life are disrupted and altered; the financial benefit of a roommate sharing expenses with him is abruptly terminated. Why did he allow it? Why were both of these men unable to go up against her? No one ever went up against her.

Once the rhythm and pattern was established, she would come with me to Florida or sometimes join me later. Was this a hidden or disguised way to leave father and still be a good person in her own mind? After all, we should be together: a mother and daughter should be together, shouldn't they?

While it had the most dire consequences for me in many ways, the irony was that my father, for whom the separation was most painful, later said, "That's what saved you." Did he regard my mother's example as unwholesome? Collisions between Mother and I had increased as I had begun to develop into womanhood.

Did she really believe that she was doing what was best for me?

Does this explain her tears?

Was this an almost Medea-like way to punish Father for his loyalty toward her when she knew she did not deserve it?

I once read somewhere the phrase, "spirit-killing rejection." Establishing this pattern in our lives, she masterfully punished and deprived herself and everyone else at the same time. Her drive to distance herself, and consequently my father and me, shows itself in every instance of our family life. We are estranged from the small number of relatives who are remnants of first generation Americans of what was a large family in the "old country."

Moats and barricades were not just intangible but existed in actual accumulations of goods and daily purchases that filled our small attic apartment. It became crowded and disorderly, and no one was admitted. From earliest times a sense of shame pervaded me if a schoolmate came "to play." Mother was powerless to do anything about it. This sense of shame was in my stomach, and in my chest, always there. It murmured behind the curtain in my sense of self. It defined me. A family secret defines you. As soon as I learned the words, I would say, "I'm sorry about the apartment." "That's OK," a friend would say. The tone of polite pity did not relieve the ache. If the doorbell rang, and Mother was there, we pretended that no one was home. That practice never ever changed.

Mother is also ashamed. Later in life, I would send flowers on her birthday or Mother's Day, until she asked me to stop. She hated the woman from the florist and didn't want to open the door to her.

After I grew up and escaped, and she became widowed, all restraints were removed. In these later years, if a neighbor knocked on the door to see if Mom was all right, and she was actually willing to open the door, it took a while to move chairs, and whatever, away from behind the door. Her progressive deafness strikes me as nature's way of participating fully in driving her into solitary confinement. All forces merge to affect a life that is not life.

Chapter 10

Florida
Miami Beach High School

A consequence of living in Florida with my grandfather during those impressionable years is that I am comfortable with older people. Will I be comfortable with myself as I join those ranks?

I remember jumping up and down on a trampoline at the Albion Hotel Cabana near the ocean end of Lincoln Road in Miami Beach. One afternoon, I spring upwards and sense instantly that I am not going to come back down on the tarp but will miss it entirely and hit the metal frame or the hard ground. Into my mind flashes a cover of a *Wonder Woman* comic book seen in my childhood, where Wonder Woman is shown performing stunts as an acrobat in the circus. As she leaps for the trapeze, an evil hand pushes it out of reach and she is meant to plummet downward. Cleverly, Wonder Woman catches the bar with her knees and, swinging upside down, she saves herself. This is exactly what I do: coming down out of the air, I slip one leg between the springs that hold the tarp to the frame and swing by one knee upside down laughing, with my long brown hair brushing the sand. Upside down, I see people, white-faced, running towards me. "It's a good thing you're an acrobat," I'm told. I feel exhilarated, but my body seems to be shaking. I have had a close call, although I will not admit that to myself.

What phenomena brought that "saving vision" to mind? I could easily have broken my neck. This memory is recalled for the first time years later in a graduate Literature course at Simmons, when discussing *Cat's Eye* by Margaret Atwood. Her child protagonist, hiding in a cold bank of water on a wintery day, has a religious vision telling her it is safe to go home now. She rescues herself.

If everything experienced or read or viewed in a film is stored in our brains, what keeps us from going mad with the quantity or randomness of what is accumulated? Perhaps not everything is "saved." Does it spin through completely, daily or nightly?

Will Wonder Woman ever save me again?

Chapter 11

Sea Gate and Sheepshead Bay

Daddy, the Crush, and the Business of Forgetting

A tender memory: I am suffering and in operatic tears because of a crush on a boy who sits at the same cafeteria table with me at Lincoln High. Mother telephones Father at work (never done before). He leaves the shop EARLY and takes the subway home to comfort me about "these feelings," as he describes them. His face is suffused with love. His eyes radiate love and tenderness. He tries to explain that these feelings will pass and are part of life and growing up. I refuse to be comforted. I wallow, I weep, I moan, I sob. In my perverse way, I am having a wonderful time. See, how important my emotions are! Daddy had to COME HOME FROM WORK. I can visualize now the other East European men in the shop at their steaming and sewing tasks. I can imagine them smiling, nodding, and sighing with remembrances of their own early stirrings of the Grand Passion. Ah, LOVE! I feel certain he was paid piece work at that time at making hats, and it cost him some wages to leave work. How disappointing my refusal to be soothed must have been for him.

The Chainlink Fence

He once told me, with visible amusement and embarrassment, that he had had plans to prepare his own translation of *Faust* and send it to Marlene Dietrich. Those echoes of *romance* made it possible for him to counsel me the way he did that afternoon, with fondness and sympathy. These are serious matters.

He had been a young man when he arrived in this country, about 23 years old. He learned English in night school, went through high school and City College. He majored in Philosophy (with an emphasis on the Greeks), all at night while working at a sewing machine during the day. One night, as he did an experiment in Chemistry Lab, the teacher approached him. "I think about you, Mr. Zuckerman," he said. "How do you do it? Work all day and then do this at night?" Father had shrugged and answered, "I don't know, inertia, I suppose." He smiled slightly as he related this memory to me, shrugging again. All that effort for his dream. Why not smile, otherwise one would weep and tear one's hair.

After I am married and gone, the little bungalow in Sheepshead Bay eventually becomes genuinely unlivable. Repairs cannot be made since no one is allowed in. "I gave up on the inside of it." Father tells me about his struggle to control the mess. "I'm just trying to keep the yard clean." Father has to force his way in at night because of what is piled up behind the door.

My parents are forced by these conditions to leave and occupy a lower Manhattan Hotel; I think his union may have subsidized the cost. If so, this would have tormented him. "Something in the mind from childhood, an innocence," he once said to me, to explain his personal code of behavior. Now he is president of a branch of the Millinery Worker's Union. Zeal for high ideals characterize all his work. He is involved in creating affordable housing for workers as well as health, pension, and welfare benefits through the union and other social action organizations.

In the bungalow's abandoned state, further decay and destruction ensue. The roof falls in. Nature and vandals leave their mark. Eventually, the bungalow is demolished by the city: a financial and emotional loss, a waste of dreams, a waste of labor. My mother is a devastating force of nature. I will never know the rationale for Father's personal inaction. He could not, or would not, save himself. He is stoic. He suffers. He becomes ill. "Whenever I think of the house, it kills me," he says. Why didn't he save himself? He did nothing in life to deserve that punishing existence. As the adult daughter, I wonder if leaving Europe when he did and not experiencing the Holocaust directly with the rest of his family made it possible, or even necessary, to endure this punishment.

One day during my junior high school years, Daddy came home from work in the steam shop, having been located by a messenger from his Polish village. The messenger had conveyed the information that none of Father's family and relatives had survived the Holocaust. My mother was quiet. I remember my father's face as he threw himself into a chair. Now looking back, I wonder about this messenger. Who was he? How did he find my father in his workshop? To whom else did he carry such messages? How had my father kept up hopes for survivors during the war years?

Among papers and photos I went through years after his death, I found an old-fashioned, very stiff cardboard, formal photograph of what must have been the family he left in the old country. The senior couple, grandparents I never knew and their adult children who would have been my aunts and uncles, are in a photographer's studio. Dark-eyed, handsome, serious young men stand behind their parents, and a beautiful young woman in a white dress is playfully posed on the ground in front of the seated old folks. I do not know their names, except for the sister: her name was Miriam, the same as my mother's. There is something in the face of the grandmother that looks familiar, especially the expression in her eyes. I think the face I see in the mirror is similar. A poignant touch: my father, who as a young man during his travels in Europe had worked as a photographer, inserts his own face from a passport picture to fit in with the row of brothers in the back row. The head is slightly larger than the other faces. Father never spoke of his people, and I did not have the sense to ask. What little I know is random bits of accidental remarks and reminiscences, inadvertently dropped. He was not talkative in general, especially not about his past. He was not in the business of remembering; he was in the business of forgetting.

He is pleased when, as a young mother, I perform in an amateur theatre group. "I acted when I was in Berlin," he said. "What part did you play?" I asked. "I was the third corner of a triangle, the other man," he says, and blushes. This is an example of how I have a small piece of information about his early life, his Odyssey as he once referred to it.

Chapter 12

Sheepshead Bay
Brooklyn College

Our threesome is reestablished in Sheepshead Bay, when I graduate from high school and begin Brooklyn College. It is the house I marry from. It is really a bungalow with a common wall in a tiny village-like locale on the bay in Brooklyn. The bay is full of fishing boats. The area looks and feels like a small harbor town in any part of the world. Plum Beach is nearby. The purchase price was, I think, $3,000.

Ineluctably, chaos begins to reappear around us as I pursue my college education. The kitchen has mice, so when I study at the kitchen table, I must keep the radio on louder than is comfortable. The loud radio makes it hard for me to concentrate but keeps the mice away.

One day in Sheepshead Bay during my college years, I wait while Mom buys a lobster from a fishing boat. She crosses the street to knock on the back door of a Chinese Restaurant. The cook quickly prepares the lobster Mandarin style and wraps it, all for 75 cents. We run home, eat, and enjoy licking our fingers. This aspect of her Bohemian nature is fun. I desire conventionality, but not this time. The lobster is delicious and makes us happy.

Since Father is in the millinery line, Mother had hundreds of hats. She looks wonderful in all of them. The way she carries herself, she looks like the Empress of all the Russias. She has a trained voice and sings around the house: opera arias, Stephen Foster songs, melancholy ballads in French and Italian, and popular ditties from the twenties. Tears come to her eyes listening to an aria on the radio. Marion Anderson is a favorite. A precious memory for mom: as a young woman, she sang in Carnegie Hall with a choir.

She had a job for a while at R.H. Macy before she was married. She spoke of being placed at the Front Counter! selling gloves. She wore a white fichu (a piece of white lace) around the neckline of her black dress. She fitted gloves on the wife of the governor of Maryland, she tells me several times over the years. And she also waited on Joan Crawford. Mom tells me of an adult camp sponsored by Macy's for employees. At the Macy's camp, she sings Taps every evening when the flag is lowered. "Come on, Miriam," the other girls would call to her.

Day is done, gone the sun
From the lakes, from the hills, from the sky
All is well, safely rest
God is nigh.

She would sing it to me. Beautiful. I had these lines carved on her tombstone when the time came to do so.

In later years, when we are limited to speaking on the phone, she tells me she is reading Turgenev's autobiography. "His description of childhood is wonderful.

Look up Byron's *Childe Harold's Pilgrimage*," she says, "It is also wonderful!" She notes particular works of gypsy music performed by James Levine that she hears on the radio. She tells me to get it, and I do.

Secondhand books were always a favorite purchase; from earliest times, strange and wonderful books exist amidst the clutter. In other ways, she cannot differentiate between something of value and beauty or secondhand clothes and costume jewelry. She speaks of fashionable fabrics from an era of couturiers: georgette, brocade, peaux de soi, crepe d'chine, panné velvet, and tulle. She has an ivory cigarette holder, mother-of-pearl opera glasses, and other luxurious accessories for an imagined life. Unreality and fantasy govern her mind with thoughts and plans. Operatic emotion is bread and butter.

There are important dictums about what is appropriate in a costume, depending on the time of day and the season of the year. She has a subscription to *Women's Wear Daily* to be up on what's coming in fashion "ahead of the season."

Anything someone has thrown away is of interest. What is the attraction to castoff goods? Why does the idea of an accidental discovery of a discarded treasure have such a powerful grip on the imagination? What is the real object of the search? She purchases broken furniture, crockery and clothing in need of repair; she plans to have it fixed and never does. Nothing is ever discarded. Items of beauty and value are mixed in with the useless and worthless. My overriding terror is to speak to her about her acquisitiveness and inability to keep purchases orderly. The victims, my father and I, are driven beyond endurance. This periodically provokes an upsetting scene, leading to defensiveness and wild counter-attack that is dreaded by everyone. Then follow weeks of silent strain.

We are in a trap: a bind of injury, of resentment, of anger, of punishment. If she reaches out to me at this time when I am in college, I harden myself. She does not seem to understand what she does to warrant this response. Now it is my turn to have power and withhold affection. My turn to have plans and to look good in clothes. As I approach graduation and become engaged, she regards me with admiration, perhaps envy. She plans the wedding. Now, now is my chance to escape. I desire conventionality. I believe firmly that I know what is right and true and important "in life."

At the Greyhound Bus Station on 42st Street one week after the wedding, my husband and I wait with our suitcases for the bus to New Jersey, where I will begin my first teaching job and the whole rest of my life. Surprise! There at the very spot, unexpectedly, are my parents and my grandmother to see us off. My reaction now as I look back and remember my response then is horror. Horror at my cruelty. How could I have mistaken their motivation? I am scared that they will not let me go, that I am not really going to be on my own. I turn my back and show my displeasure. I can still see their eyes looking happy to see me, then shocked and surprised at my displeasure, and finally, hurt, very hurt. My father is particularly hurt. Grandma says, "Moma made it happen we should see you." Her eyes show disbelief at my coldness. I hear my mother say to my grandmother, "She doesn't like surprises, that's all." Mother tried to excuse and explain me and herself, because "her plan" did not produce the result, or the reception, she had anticipated.

    I cause pain.

Chapter 13

Brighton Beach
"Sadie, Sadie, Married Lady"

After a long absence and through almost random circumstance, I visit my parents in Brighton Beach for a few hours. I am stunned at the intensity of recollections and sensations that sweep over and through me, generated by the characteristic smells of the ocean side in high summer and, in particular, the fragrance from the wood of the boardwalks.

When it is time for my departure, they walk me to the Brighton Beach stop on the BMT subway. In order to prolong our moments together, my father buys himself a token for the subway to be with me on the outdoor platform while I wait for the train that will take me to midtown Manhattan. From there, I will catch a bus to Princeton and will connect, the following day, with my husband who is attending a meeting there. My mother waits on the street. "A daughter visits and can't stay over," Father says bitterly.

As I look toward the crowds on the street below the subway platform, I say to my father, out of my mouth, matter-of-factly, and with a private just-between-us tone, "I feel above these people." "You are, you are," he responds, without hesitation and with some emotion.

The next moment, a pleasant looking senior gentleman taps me on the shoulder and hands me a brown paper bag. "Here, this is from your mother," he says smiling. Mystified, I ask, "How did you know it was meant for me?" He continues to smile, enjoying the little Bohemian episode. "Your mother said, 'Give this to my daughter, she's the good looking girl,'" he responds as he walks away. Inside the small bag are cookies from a local bakery. My father and I look at each other sharing a moment of exasperation at her eccentricities. We shake our heads, commiserating.

The Nassau Inn at Princeton is the snootiest of the snooty—the last word in upper-class appointments and demeanor. I go to my reserved room, freshen up, return to the lobby, and ask for the dining room. "The dining room is closed. Dinner has been served," I am informed. Taken aback, I say, "All right, where is the coffee shop?" I can make do with a sandwich if I must. "There is no coffee shop," I am told, aloofly. I return to my room; the contents of the small brown bag with a drink of water is my dinner.

Two things happened in those brief moments for which I am unable to forgive myself. I am simply ashamed of what I said to my father, and I know for a fact that I was wrong. Yes, the thrust of those times was to elevate oneself— through education—to emulating the established and successful, but I now know "those people," as I referred to them, are far better than I.

When I hear those diphthongs and glottal stops

these days, I feel I am hearing the truth. When someone speaks in polished tones or elite accents, I have a vague sense that I am being lied to or finessed in some way. This is somewhat of an exaggeration, but not by much.

What Mother sent in that wrinkled paper bag was love.

I betrayed it.

Chapter 14

Lincoln, Massachusetts
Nana Mary

During the year we lived in Lincoln, Massachusetts, Mother agrees to come from Brooklyn for three whole weeks to babysit. She makes it possible for me to travel to Paris. Three weeks is a very long time. She is happy for me that I have the opportunity. When she has a letter from me and sees the French postmark, she cannot get over it. "My girl made it!" she says. She takes excellent care of the children and tells me when I return of a spontaneous kiss given by my baby girl and how special that was. "I won't forget it," she says. I can picture it easily as Mother describes it. My little girl stands on the changing table, Mother brushes her soft hair and the baby reaches her arms around Mother's neck and kisses her. It is a loving act for Mother to come and save the day for me. I had spent endless fruitless hours trying to find a babysitter.

While in Paris, I dream one night that my grandmother is standing next to my hotel bed. She looks as she looked when I was a little girl, not as she does now, frail and aged.

Upon returning, we received a call from my father saying that during my time away, grandma did die. "Be strong, be strong," he tells Mother on the phone. He and Mother's two brothers had attended to everything without informing my mother. He justifies this act on the grounds that she is caring for my children. The message is clear to me. While her child care responsibilities are a major factor (he would not want to discombobulate the children), Mother's participation would have made it harder and a strain on the three men. It was a relief to make the decisions without her. When I tell him I had anticipated my grandmother might die and had backup plans, he rightfully queries, "With all those calls you made, why didn't you make one more and inform me?" I had no answer. Now I suspect an unconscious motivation. I must have wanted to make sure my mother would not be called away. Another act for which I must find expiation!

Mysteriously, Mother never reproached me. She refers to these events as "How It Happened" (that she was not there), and says "I will have to wait till I see Grandma to explain."

In later years she tells me on the phone, "She's very close, I feel Grandma very close to me, Naomi."

Chapter 15

Brighton Beach
Abandoned Accounts

I am dropped off on Brighton Beach Avenue. I walk to the corner across from the Lincoln Savings Bank. At a loss, I wonder, "What am I doing here?"

Waves of familiarity sweep over me: the fragrance of the ocean air, the voices and street life, the strange yet recognizable faces, and the Russian accents. Many, many elderly persons, not so much evident poverty, not low-life's, yet many unstable persons mixed in the crowd. An overall and pervasive sense of the struggle for existence; the avenue and the side streets all bordered with fruit stalls and food shops. To live is to eat. Food overflows the sidewalk bins, and bodies flow in and around the displays: touching, sniffing, scrutinizing, and selecting.

I systematically begin my task, going to four banks all near each other. It is my intention to clear up the "Abandoned Account" status of my mother's accounts. "She is not deceased," I say. The bankers are generally sympathetic and understanding. "You are trying to help from the outside," one says. Each time I am out on the avenue, I gaze up at the kitchen window of #500 to the 14th floor where my mother is barricaded in her apartment. I look at the window. I feel an intense connection, confusion and fright. I shake. I put my hand on the receiver of a pay phone to call and ask if I can come up to see her. I am unable to lift the receiver. I tremble, feel weak, and am overcome with intense waves of longing and fear. I ask directions to the fourth bank, which is on Neptune Avenue. I walk there. Each of those four conversations is very emotional.

Back on the avenue, I become hungry and need a bathroom. The luncheonette where I have my sandwich has no bathroom facilities. Nowhere on the avenue is a bathroom available; I see I must use the public toilet in the subway station. With trepidation I fling open the door of the Women's. There are two stalls. As I enter, an angry face darts out of one cubicle, scowling. She is busy with what seems to be several bundles. I feel at risk, even menaced because of her hostile expression, but I must "go." As I crouch over the commode, my eyes are riveted to my ankle where I expect to be shot, struck a blow, or otherwise seized. This episode adds to the terror and nightmarish unreality of the day. At the same time, it feels more real. *Everything* seems more real than it is.

I arrange car-service at a street-front location of the utmost squalor. Nailed up planks on the dirty walls have white painted letters explaining the terms of charges. All of this time, as the hours of the day slip by, Mother is within reach. I am assigned a Russian driver who speaks little English. He never heard of the Waldorf Astoria.

I write the words on a piece of paper, and he calls the dispatcher for directions.

Arriving at the Waldorf Astoria, I enter opulence. I go to my room, and bathe, rest, change, and join my husband to go to the posh East Side restaurant La Biche for a deluxe meal and service. Mother's presence surrounds me. That evening among the festive and elite diners, I think of where I had been and what emotions had flooded me earlier that day. I feel battered, even crazy. Was I the same person? I have always felt solitude, isolation, aloneness in and from a world not of my own making and, once again, I feel my powerlessness to affect it.

Chapter 16

Brighton Beach
Cards and Notes

She has been living her own life. We speak on the phone often but do not see each other. I call for motherly "life advice," and it seems to me she gives me good counsel. Once during my quest for work, I am led to a part time job by a Boston museum director, who tells me he wishes me to be grateful for the favor. He persists; I feel vulnerable. Troubled, not tempted yet confused, I ask Mother what to do. "Don't give yourself!" she admonishes me, her voice strong over the wires from Brooklyn to Boston. I feel relief at her certainty. I feel well advised.

She enjoys my notes and letters, as well as greetings from foreign lands when I travel. I send a wicked little postcard from Italy. It shows the naked baby boy water fountain in Boboli Gardens in Florence that has water spouting from his nether-regions. She laughs about it when I see her. She didn't want the postman to see it, she said, her eyes sparkling. A card from Rome showing a satyr sipping wine, eyes gleaming with bacchanalian joy and inviting the viewer to whom the cup is lifted to participate in the revels. This I later see pasted up on her apartment wall. One card from Sicily I compose in Italian: *Cara Mama, Tutto e squisito, Con Amore*, Naomi. She tells me every saved note she rereads is like a little visit from me.

Back home, I increase the flow of notes and cards with beautiful paintings from Boston museums. On the phone, I describe the large golden statue of Diana that had graced the top of a New York building, now on exhibit at the Boston Museum of Fine Arts. I describe a performance by Judith Jamison in a ballet created by the choreographer Alvin Ailey for his mother's birthday and dedicated to "mothers everywhere." I describe the costume, music, choreography, and emotion. "Go, go! See, see!" She encourages me. I visualize her shaking her head from side to side in approval.

Time passes in this way.

During two days in Manhattan, I visit the Van Gogh exhibit at the Metropolitan. I have no ticket so I follow the advice of the ticket-taker and stand with a hand-lettered sign on a yellow legal pad saying, "Out-of-towner wants ticket to show." Quickly a woman sells me an extra she has. Once inside, I enjoy myself and buy a poster for Mother in the gift shop.

The next morning when I call to say I am planning to take the subway to see her, she makes every effort to dissuade me by urging me to walk on Fifth Avenue and enjoy "The Windows," something she had always enjoyed. I will not be dissuaded. The trip on the train is further heightened in intensity by the presence of a disturbed man in my subway car. He is very small. He stands ranting, dressed in a blue military jacket, addressing, I think, an absent person and making threats. "Don't put your spit on me, woman!" he shrieks. No one else seems perturbed or affected; I am terrified. Of the other people in the car, I look the most prosperous, wearing my fur coat from Filene's Basement to show Mother. I feel certain that I will be the likely object of any violence or anger. As we rattle over the bridge from Manhattan to Brooklyn, I sweat in fear. I think I will never again see the people I care about in life. At the next stop, I run out and into the next car down.

During the visit to Mother, I thumbtack the poster of black-limbed apple blossoms on a blue sky to her bedroom wall so she can see it from her bed. I glimpse it still on the wall years later when I attempt to clean out the apartment after she is no longer present.

Chapter 17

Brighton Beach
On the 14th Floor

Gradually Mother is more and more fearful of being seen. She opens the apartment door just a crack and carefully peers out to determine that the corridor is empty. She then nods and closes the door.

Something tumor-like grows on her face; she will not see a doctor. She has lost her bridgework, yet refuses dental care. Instead of going out only at night to shop, she now hides completely from sight. She does not leave the apartment at all. If the telephone rings; she doesn't answer. The theme is it's everyone else's fault that she has come to this dreadful pass: the social worker whom she had trusted, the neighbors…mostly, it's me. Any attempt that I make to say anything is not allowed. I am screamed down. Angrily she says, "I understand you are in touch with a friend of mine." She refers to Sherri, the social worker from Protective Services Agency. The PSA is the last recourse for elderly people in the hierarchy of city agencies.

I had arranged for Sherri's visits, and I confer with her regularly. Mother asks why I am interfering in her life. I am the enemy. She tells Sherri, "Naomi gives the impression of being a concerned daughter, but really it's the money she is interested in." When asked by a visiting health care person from Coney Island Hospital how she feels about me, her only child, she answers, "Numb." Another time she said, "I don't want Naomi to see me like this." She never says she hates me, Sherri tells me. Some comfort.

Now I keep even closer contact with Sherri and with Charlotte, mother's neighbor who is also the 14th floor captain. The captain of each floor in the building "checks" on the aged apartment dwellers if they have not been seen for two or three days. Other duties include collection for the "Super's" Xmas gift, receiving complaints, and managing other important responsibilities in the life of the building. Relief floods me when she agrees to shop for Mother. I send checks and call every other day or so to speak with Charlotte in detail about Mother's condition. She reports on conversations that they have together when Mother finally opens the door to Charlotte's knocking. The effect on everyone is nerve wracking. I worry. Charlotte tries to satisfy Mother's particular food requirements. Mother wants sweet potatoes, bananas, grapes, and bread. The potatoes must match in size; grapes must be black, not green; most of all, the bread must be two-day-old dark Russian. There is yelling if the bread is fresh and full price. Mom's other neighbor calls to tell me Mom has good "Rappaport" with Sherri, the social worker.

Sherri had tried to persuade Mother to take meals-on-wheels and a home companion, which are available to her. All offers of assistance are refused. There is an official shopping service I speak with. To avail yourself of it, the client must give "Information!" Charlotte explains to me. None of the ladies in the building, even Charlotte, will agree to give "Information." This circumstance continues for a long time. Mother will not allow anyone in. If something breaks, the toilet, the refrigerator, it remains that way, and she adapts.

I embark on the task of replacing the fridge. It takes months of planning because I must work around the rules of the co-op and finesse all usual procedures. All because she will not let in anyone from the building. The morning I catch a 7 AM flight from Boston to Kennedy Airport to wait for the delivery, I think to myself, if there is a new working refrigerator in place in her kitchen when I return this evening, it will be a miracle. Success! For weeks after, I am elated at having improved her life, if only that much. When we speak on the phone, she asks, "How did they know I like eggs so much?" about the cute little spots, just for eggs. "A bride wouldn't have anything nicer," she tells me.

Subsequently, any contact between us is devastating for us both and I stop calling, relying on the two other contacts I have. The only effect I can have is to try to make sure she is not hungry. I am loath to institutionalize her; Charlotte and I believe that would kill her. Many times Mother has expressed dread of relinquishing her independence. I feel unable to go against those wishes and, especially, not to be in an adversarial mode of any kind toward her. Her reproaches terrify me.

Charlotte reports Mother's physical condition is deteriorating. She continues to refuse to be taken to a doctor. "If I go to a doctor, he'll put me in the hospital." A sudden further loss of weight alarms us all. Sherri gets a promotion and is no longer "in the field," and some new man is placed in the position of trying to win Mother's confidence so she will open the door. Then Charlotte becomes ill and is unable to shop any longer. I exhaust all further avenues of aid. There is no choice but to remove her, and this must be done forcibly since she refuses all offers of help. The social worker, Charlotte, the contact I have at Coney Island Hospital, and my counselor all advise me not to be present as it is thought that this will make it harder for Mother who will see me yet again as the enemy.

Ironically, events unfold so that it is December 22nd when all papers and persons are ready, and Mother is taken by ambulance to Coney Island Hospital. I am aware all day of the events as I visualize the 14th floor of her building. I picture the three policemen, the psychiatrist, and the locksmith who will break in, if necessary, and will secure the lock after she is out. Most of all, I picture what I imagine are the reactions and shock of this frail, disturbed elderly woman. As she is taken down in the elevator in a wheelchair, Charlotte tells me Mother is heard to repeat, "I don't need a hospital, I don't need a hospital."

Once I learn she is in the hospital, I feel relief. She is "in the system." She will finally get attention and care; I expect she will need lengthy attention. "This woman is charming," says the man in the gurney next to Mother, the hospital social worker tells me. The winter holiday complicates the hospital services; there is crowding, and the staff is overworked. I learn that elderly family members are sent to the emergency room by their relatives so they are not around and the family can go on holiday or celebrate without them.

After three days, I receive astonishing news from the hospital! Mother must leave. Why? Because there is nothing wrong with her! Dehydrated, yes. Mental confusion, yes. But absolutely no physical sickness, illness or condition of any kind whatsoever. She will not be admitted: no medicines or treatments are indicated. Mom was right, she did not need a hospital.

I cannot bear to return her to neglect and isolation. She cannot live alone. I accept the prospect of a nursing home. I choose one in Sheepshead Bay, just a few blocks from the bungalow we once owned when I was in college. This way she can continue to be near the ocean she loves. However, a mistake is made, and she is sent to the wrong nursing home while I am in the insane situation of being on a holiday celebration with friends at Asilomar on the California coast for New Year's weekend. My entire being is focused on the events occurring on another coast. I think of nothing else. There is no phone for me to use. A new style phone in the dining area that takes a charge card for billing baffles me as I try and am unable to use it. I am miserable and shaken.

By the time I arrive in Brooklyn on January $2^{nd,}$ in addition to all of the other issues and tasks I confront, I must also decide if the mistake should be corrected and I should have her moved again to the nursing home by the ocean. My overriding concern, however, is emotional and overwhelms everything else. Will she see me, and if she does, will I be denounced and vilified?

My Mother
Miriam Rabinowitz Zuckerman
October 16, 1905 – August 27, 2000

Chapter 18

Coney Island Avenue
Nursing Home

I walk down the tiled corridor of the nursing home, glancing oh-so-carefully into each room on either side to see if I recognize my 89-year-old mother. My daughter Natalie is with me. It is too long since I have seen Mother. Although we spoke on the phone almost daily, that too ended when she decided I was interfering in her life.

Elderly persons as well as obviously abnormal persons are about, some walking, most in wheelchairs. I am holding my breath. Mental disturbance is as prevalent as physical abnormality. Most of the patients are women; they seem to resemble each other. Sunken bodies, sparse fly-away wispy hair, lump-like physicality are the most shared attributes. Faces look like pasty muffin dough that could be easily formed and reformed. Chests and rib cages seem to have disappeared, evaporated or erased, along with pride. They stare at me; the stare is not friendly. I pursue my search. One elderly woman in a wheelchair has Tourette's syndrome and calls out obscenities. "Are you Jewish?" she screams at me. "You f-----g Jew," she keeps yelling after I pass. No one seems to notice or pay attention. *"Abandon all hope ye who enter here."*

I pass a wheelchair in a doorway with a small, emaciated woman who has a towel over her face. I glance at her, then I gaze steadily in her direction. I feel something, I don't know what. All I see is the tiny body and the short, very short, white hair. My mother has long hair, of which she is proud! I continue searching in fear of what I will find.

Sheets of tears are covering my face, although I am making every effort not to cry. "Stop crying, stop crying," the head nurse tells me. I tell the nurse I cannot find my mother. She says, "I'll wheel her to her room and then you can go in." She goes to the chair that holds the woman with the towel covered face and wheels her past me. "You have company," the nurse says to the patient. That is how I know that the emaciated woman in the wheelchair is my mother. She is groaning.

The tears keep coming as I stand in the hall trying to control myself. I have the necessary moment to strengthen myself and adjust to the shock of seeing her as skin and bones. Her hair has been drastically cut. They were unable to untangle it to wash when she arrived. It *had* to be cut. Miracle of miracles, she is matter-of-fact about seeing me. She does not remember that she is supposed to be angry at me. We speak, and she asks about former friends.

For the rest of the week, I visit her every day. She is traumatized about the forcible removal from her apartment to The Home. She keeps referring to what happened, yet is totally accepting of her surroundings;

nor does she question how or why she is there. She accepts my words and gestures of love with shining eyes, even makes a few jokes and takes in what I am wearing. She tells Natalie to turn around so she can study her outfit. Natalie turns slowly; Mother approves, nods, and says, "I always loved red."

When I ask if she wants anything, she emphasizes her wish with intense arm gestures: "I want strong, black coffee." After supper one night, a tall, young black man comes around with a thermos of hot coffee and Styrofoam cups. "Hi, handsome," she says when she looks up at him.

One evening as I leave, an Asian patient pulls on my arm and leads me into her room, talking rapidly in Chinese. She shows me her dresser top, speaking and pointing. I do not know what she wants; I smile and nod but cannot be any help. I am careful to avoid her when I return. What special torment to speak and not be understood. What marvels of torment exist in finer and finer forms of desperation.

As I say good night, Mother tells me, "I don't like the 'reaks' with an F, and now I'm one of them." She then moves her lips in prayer, saying the *Shema*. I feel an agony of heartbreak to see her like this, confused and physically deteriorated. She has no medical problems. None! Needs no medication. Has no physical ailment, only mental. (Only?)

On Friday evening, I wheel mother to the Sabbath service. The room is full of wheelchairs; many disturbed and lump-like persons are strapped in to keep from falling. Patients are crying out. One woman has to be removed because the disturbance is too great, but the Rabbi still tries to conduct the service. It is Sabbath service in Bedlam.

Meanwhile Mother seems to think it is some kind of show and is tapping her feet to the piano music. Standing behind her wheelchair, I feel again the sheets of tears on my face. The Rabbi notices. After he is done, he walks off the bemah and speaks to me, "It is hard to put a parent in A Home." He reassures me that the staff is skilled and he offers help. I ask for Mother to be in a two-person room instead of a four-person room. He arranges it. Consistent as ever, she complains during the change that I have made some decision on her behalf.

I have been bringing her grapes, of which she is fond. "Yummy, yum," she says the first time. She reports enjoying being fed gefilte fish. She lets me massage her head. I don't want to be away from her. She begins to urge me to leave and go back. "I'm comfortable," she tells me. That is eloquent for her because she would never not have a complaint. I drop one more grape in her mouth as she lies on the bed ready for sleep. "It's getting dark. Ske'daddle," she says.

I ske'daddle back to California.

On the phone long distance, she tells me the food is the finest. Rifka, the head social worker, tells me Mother is feeding herself now and gaining weight; she eats with the other "guests." She is ambulatory with assistance. Evidently that is a big difference in category. She can go to the toilet with help; another big difference in category.

When I speak with her on the phone, she calls me "dear" and asks about the family and sends greetings, but when I tell her I love her, she will not respond in kind. Very consciously she evades those words. "You always did, in your way," she answers. She holds back from me what I want; I want her to say she loves me. As she speaks she is lucid, her voice calm, the diction perfect, the tone deliberate and in control. Ever the adversary. Still holding out. I am bad, I interfere. A good, strong yank on my chain.

She reports on receiving her bath and telling the attendant, "You do all the work, and I'm the one who is tired!"

Still with the wise-cracks.

Chapter 19

Coney Island Nursing Home
Entertainment and Straw Hats

Visiting Mother in the Nursing home back in Brooklyn on Coney Island Avenue, we are unexpectedly called outside for "Entertainment." It takes me a moment to wheel the chair outside onto the fenced cement area in front of the building.

It is the first time in my life I have ever touched a wheelchair, and Mother is in it. There is a feeling of shock, taking the handles in my hands. There is something familiar about it. It evokes something else; I cannot think what it is. Suddenly I am stung by the similarity between the materials that make the wheelchair and those of Mother's bike: the chrome tubing and wheels, the rubber tires, the handles covered with plastic grips. Mother was known as the "Lady on the Bike" when I was growing up. She never drove a car and did all marketing on her bike. She put me on the back, behind her, on a makeshift seat. An unusual practice then and deeply humiliating to me.

It is May, and in front of the nursing home, a few young trees give some shade. All the wheelchairs are placed in rows side by side. It is hot and sunny and folks are out walking the Avenue. On the other side of the railing in the road, cars and trucks pass. Commerce, activity, noise, bearded men in black suits, and youths, also in black suits despite the warmth walk jauntily. There are many young mothers with baby strollers. Mother comments on each passerby's personality as revealed by their "walk."

Two frail elderly men confer in the small space in the middle of the fenced-in area. There is a keyboard on metal legs covered with a white towel. "You know it has be in the shade. Last year we were on the other side." Angry looks and gestures about the necessity of keeping the keyboard cool and out of the sun.

Meanwhile because of the heat, each immobile, small, and still person is topped off with a straw cowboy hat. From where I sit toward the back with my mother, it looks like the wheelchairs are wearing hats. The hats do not move. The two frail men stop arguing and address the wheelchairs—all charm and smiles—and begin a song and joke routine straight out of the Borscht Belt. *They* are the "Entertainment."

The songs are oldies but goodies: *Come to the Cabaret, Tura Lura,* and something about *the girls I've loved and left.* The singer has a polished, strong voice. The tempo is lively. The patter between singer and keyboard player is automatic, worn smooth by years of repetition. When the music begins, the straw hats move, and almost immediately they lift up and bob from side to side in time to the music. Cracked voices say the words. One slender lady gets up from her chair and wiggles her hips and claps. She is wearing beads around her neck; they swing to the beat. Others join. The mood is buoyant.

Mother sings a few lines and smiles.

There are smiles that make me happy,
There are smiles that make me gay,
But the smiles that fill my heart with sunshine
Are the smiles that you give to me.

We both enjoy ourselves. I sit on a bench against the brick wall holding Mother's wheelchair very close and prop my feet on the wheelchair's metal leg supports. Passersby stop, lean on the iron railing, smile, sing along, and greet the wheelchairs with waves and more smiles and "Hi's." Mom points out a tiny newborn on a mother's shoulder. "Cute," she whispers. The mother jiggles the baby in time to the music.

I feel a strange bliss, the first such relief in a long while. I want never to leave.

Chapter 20

Coney Island Nursing Home
Balloons

"Your mother is basking in the things you have sent her," said Rifka when I ask, "How is she? How's she doing?" The social worker's reassuring words are precious to me as they slide over the phone wires to California from Brooklyn. I ballooned Mom with helium balloons. They last longer than any other kind. "I LOVE YOU, HAPPY MOTHER'S DAY" they were supposed to exclaim. Last time the balloons did not get all the way down the corridor to her room but stayed in the front reception area. This year I phone to make certain she actually receives them.

The florist is on Avenue J, the nursing home is between Avenues K and L. It should be a small matter to deliver them. Evidently the messenger delivers only to the front desk. Perhaps walking the gauntlet down the linoleum-covered floors, smelling the pervasive, piercing odor of urine and equally powerful cleanser and deodorizer is not to his liking.

The shock, the emotional impact, the sense of descending into a nether region separate from the outside world was crystallized by the odor the first time

I had entered this other world, this drowned Atlantis under the surface of normal life. Outside, folks shop and hurry, pre-occupied as they are with daily tasks, while here, here is a meta-reality codified by this suffocating odor. This is real. The outside world is the childhood of life, innocence, unknowing playacting and pretense, the necessary concealment of truth. Yes, necessary.

The odor greets me on my subsequent returns, but curiously it now welcomes me; it is no longer unpleasant. Oh, yes, I have arrived. I am there, I think. An animal sensory response. Yes, yes I am exactly here. The house staff and aides are spotless in their whites. Floors are continuously mopped. Never an un-made bed. Patients (residents?) are always dressed and upright in chairs, even if they are unaware. The office staff, I am certain, is encouraged to dress fashionably even glamorously. They are made-up and look chic. The effect is reassuring. No doubt as it is meant to be. I am never sure how friendly and communicative to be with the nurses and aides. I sense they are not pleased about caring for the old and infirm members of families who are not able to care for their own. The unease and distance I feel is further enhanced by their island accents: Haitian, Jamaican, and similar lilts.

Years earlier, attending a Thanksgiving gathering in Manhattan, my mother is invited by my in-laws as a courtesy to me. My younger sister-in-law, Linda, who is institutionalized, is present. She is accompanied by another young women, clearly a trained caretaker whose participation makes it possible for Linda to be with her family. Both pretty girls are in their late 20's; the Patient and her Caretaker. Mother is the only person who speaks with this young caretaker. Across the room, I see Mother shake her head from side to side, then nod up and down. I recognize this response. She is impressed and touched by this girl's work and history. As for myself and the other guests, we pretend the caretaker is not there. Only my mother is able to acknowledge that particular reality.

Now Mother is surrounded by caretakers. As for reality, she asks me how long she has been in this place. When I hold up three fingers she shakes her head in denial. When she asks how old she is, I write 92 in the notebook I have provided for her for remembering things. She shakes her head from side to side, smiling, rejecting, and denying.

When I prepare to depart and make the return trip home to California, I take her hands and kiss each fingertip. She is touched. She smiles and says, "Naomi, you're embarrassing me." Her parting words are, "Be discreet. Have discretion in life."

Am I indiscreet in writing about her?

Chapter 21

Coney Island Nursing Home
Night Visit

Some time after Mother's Day, I visit, going directly from the airport to arrive around 8 pm on a summer's evening. Soft air, summer blue velvet sky. I find the room dark and the two frail roommates asleep for the night. Shock! I stand riveted in the doorway. I must take in the sight of raised bed rails on each metal bed. Eventually I enter and sit in a chair right next to the pillow where Mother's head rests. The only light is from the nurses' station in the hall. I slip my hand through the bars and hold Mother's hand as she sleeps. Eloquence other than mine is needed to express the silence, the circumstance, those thoughts, and those sensations that flood through me. Shortly she wakes. She is startled at seeing me, but not excessively so. It is as if I materialized out of her dreams.

Holding my hand, she denounces the surroundings, the staff, and the care. "They treat you like a dog," she says. "They are all smiles, but they are not what they seem." I am silent. The sight of the railings has made me numb.

As she speaks, I think of a story by Professor Nabokov in which he relates his travels by train to sit at the bedside of an unconscious, dying friend and colleague. When daylight arrives, he sees his vigil was at the side of a stranger; he sat all night in the wrong room. As he returns home to work and teach that day, he reflects that the error was not important, not actually relevant to his purpose.

And I? How do I process the circumscribing of Mother's life? Metal railings are her parameters. How to accept the erasure of her vista, the narrowing of her horizons to those railings, bed, bathroom, sink, and one window? All her belongings in one small drawer. Her life and her space is bounded by iron poles, wherever she may be in her dreams.

Chapter 22

Manhattan: 86th and Broadway
The Subway

In June I return again to visit Mother, passing through Philadelphia to spend two days with my daughter. On Sunday I take the Amtrak from Philly to Manhattan, drop my gear, and connect briefly with my son on West 86th Street. Memories return of my former life when married to his father. We arrange for our evening meal before I leave to visit Mother. He does not express the wish to accompany me nor do I ask him.

In an attack of economy or stinginess, I take the D train for the cost of a token, $1.25, to save car service or taxi fare. It should be quick and easy to get to the Avenue J station in the Midwood section of Brooklyn. I am unaware that Sunday schedules are different. Express trains do not run; furthermore on Sunday, repairs are made on the tracks and detours are routine. What should take 25 minutes takes 1 ½ hours. The slow movement adds to my stress. Will I ever get there? The D train at 86th street, where I got on, goes to 59th, where a change is made to a train going to 34th, there a local Q train inches along through Brooklyn to Avenue J.

On the last segment of the trip, an argument develops between two women. Arguments terrify me. I fear I will be drawn into a violent quarrel against my wishes. This one develops over the screaming of a baby who has been shrieking non-stop, ignored by the mother. "He will get a hernia from crying!" says the concerned woman. "I'm a nurse," she tells me, in an aside. "He's teething," screeched the mother. I am seated near the argument and put my hand up to my head. The concerned woman accuses the other of giving "the lady" (me) a headache. The retort comes back, "the lady can move her seat."

I leap from the train at my stop and join the throngs on the streets. I feel I have escaped from danger. The neighborhood is full of Sunday afternoon shoppers, all Orthodox Jews. Women have their heads covered. They push babies in strollers, hold toddlers by the hand, and seem to be "expecting," all at the same time. I am among folks different from me, yet I now feel safe. I am no longer confined and in danger; no one is screaming.

The visit goes well although I feel limp from the roller coaster ride of the day's changing surroundings and emotions. I take car-service back to 86th Street where my son and I walk to Broadway and buy take-out dinner. Chicken, hot mashed potatoes, and cole slaw. All good. This neighborhood has a different ambiance; the population is urbane and prosperous. I feel plunged into yet another world. We carry our dinner back, eat together, and talk. I am happy to be with my son. Was I in Philly that same morning? Did I feel at risk on the subway? I did see my Mother again. How is it possible, all in one day?

Chapter 23

Coney Island Nursing Home
New York Times

Amidst the sustained chaos, she sat quietly, neatly, cleanly with hair brushed back becomingly. Even a shadow of her former beauty flickered in her face and her bearing. The newspaper folded neatly in front of her; she was studying an article deeply. She told me it was on race relations between blacks and whites. She held the folded paper sideways to screen her lips as she dropped her voice to a whisper, so the black staff would not hear.

When I asked if she would prefer a large print edition, she said, "No, they don't have the same good writers." The newspapers were stacked a foot high on the night table. Rifka, the head social worker, said, "she's hoarding them." Mother was so pleased with receiving a daily paper. She clearly knew I arranged it, and I think she believes I personally mail them to her.

With only one good eye and scanning with the eye glasses from her drawer, she reads with concentration, screening out the surroundings, the noise, the blathering. With wrecked nobility, astonishing intelligence, and lively humor she says, "This little bottle from my dinner tray says, 'Shake Well'." She shakes herself, laughing—

"Shake well," she giggles. "It's a miracle I'm still here. Someone is looking out for me," pointing upward.

She continues to thrive, gain weight, laugh, and make jokes. Her beautiful hair grows in. "Your mother looks like Marie Antoinette," the aide says. "Who's the famous painter, Blackwell, Norman Blackwell?"

"Do you mean Norman Rockwell?"

"Yes, that's who. That's who should paint her."

I am reassured by the comment. So kindly and genuinely offered.

Chapter 24

Brooklyn and Manhattan

Swan Lake

The male lead dancing the prince in Swan Lake is clear to me today, although I watched him float and leap over sixty years ago. My parents are seated on either side of me—their very young and only child. "He is more graceful than the women," Father says during intermission. Mother and I exchange a knowing glance. *We know* why he is more graceful. We know.

Yes, yes, I think, what grace, magic, and beauty: the black tunic, the white tights, the collar and flowing bow! Ah, fantasy! Ah, dreams of love! My life awaits future rapture in the fairy tales. It is surely only a matter of time.

Although my parents lived in a five story walk up in Greenwich Village, I was born in Brooklyn. Mother tells me how she would sit in Washington Square Park with me, a newborn in my baby carriage, right next to the building where Mrs. Eleanor Roosevelt lived. Mother wanted me to have Brooklyn on my birth certificate. I also have it on my college diploma. I left Brooklyn by the classic "Up escalator of life—marriage," but that is another story.

Later on when I am in grade stool, on a school night Mom and Dad take me into the city. We go to a fancy

The Chainlink Fence

hotel to see and hear Mrs. Roosevelt. The chairs had been arranged ahead of time for us to sit on. She addresses the attentive, assembled men and woman from the Millinary Workers Union. The only line I remember is when she struck her hand down hard on the podium for emphasis. Her voice rose, "It is *here* in the rank and file of the labor movement that…"

I marveled, how did she know that? How did she know that these were the folks that she was actually talking to right then?

But this story is about ballet class.

Not until I was in college and had some control over my life choices did I begin taking ballet classes on 8th Avenue and 48th Street with Jean Hamilton, a Bostonian who had danced with the Ballet Russe de Monte Carlo. How magical that sounded! Although a tiny woman, she had wonderful carriage and a regal air. What stern elegance! What principles! "Oh no, I walk in the front door and pay full price," she said when offered the opportunity to purchase something wholesale through an adult student. She had, as well, the exotic accessory of a horse of her own, which she kept stabled in Central Park.

My motivation to start dancing actually came from the deepest source, a broken heart. A boy whom I cared for had gone away and did not write to me. I would become accomplished and then … then he would know what he had lost.

Saturday morning and two nights a week, I took the BMT from Sheepshead Bay to Manhattan. I walked from

Broadway down 48th Street to 8th Avenue and up three flights of stairs to the top floor studio. Music, castanets, clicking heels, or singing streamed from each studio. One morning there was excitement because Lawrence Melchior was rehearsing there.

    The ballet studio had a wooden floor, an upright piano, high mirrored walls, and old fashioned narrow windows that could slide up or down to open or close even though they were as tall as the room. One cold, rainy morning when the windows fogged with condensed steam, I wrote my name on the glass with my fingertip. One of the dancers said if I worked hard for, say ten years, I could succeed professionally. Adding 10 to 17 was 27; that seemed too late to be anything. Too old, I had missed my opportunity!

Chapter 25

Boston and Palo Alto
"Mess It Up"

I returned to a dance studio after a 15 year hiatus. From that moment on, I continued to dance the years away. By then, I had been an army wife, taught school all over the U.S., and became a mother. Each baby was a pin on their father's academic trail map: Princeton, Cornell, MIT, and Harvard. I had indeed left Brooklyn, I thought! (One memento of Brooklyn College remains: I never stopped reading thick novels by English women writers.) Here at Stanford University, my nest has no chickadees. Brooklyn pulls me from another source: my mother is still there. I have not escaped. That, too, is another story.

Robecheau, the French Canadian ballet master in Boston, was memorable on several counts. Entering his brick home on Charles Street in Boston was like stepping into a now vanished Degas world. The studio on the first floor had a full length oil painting of him when young, on his toes in relevé with his arms over his head in high fifth position. It loomed like an altar piece. "The shrine," he laughingly called it. The fair hair was now grey; age and indulgence could not be concealed. Yet something happened when he moved his debauched, overweight, and ill body across the floor, demonstrating a combination. Something exciting and theatrical! When he requested more complicated choreography than usual, and it was time to move across the floor solo, we all became paralyzed. He would call out, "Go on, mess it up, mess it up! Get out there and disgrace yourself!" He gave permission to fail.

I think about his admonition to "mess it up." When I try to decide what to do in some life-affecting situation, I hear his voice. I told my children that particular adage. My son used it to audition successfully for a high school play; my daughter thought of it numerous times in matters of the heart.

In "Robie's" office, stuck on the telephone in his handwriting, I saw penciled a small note: "Charisma! Majesty! You have it!" Who would think of such a thing? A small, amusing bit of vanity, yet I wonder about it. What would I pencil on a note stuck on the phone about myself? What would I say?

I still take ballet classes. When the music is especially beautiful or poetic; when I happen to get something right; when mind, spirit, and body connect, I feel Mother watching and nodding approval. Even stranger, when I am clumsy and blank out a combination or feel discouraged, I sense her encouraging me. Where does that come from? The encouragement? Would it be because that is the single area where we were most connected? It is the aesthetic and artistic sensibility that we shared. It was the one attribute I was receptive to that she cultivated in me in her eccentric way.

When Robie became fatally ill, I held his hand at the bedside in the hospital but he did not know me. Staring straight ahead, he saw something only he could see. His face suffused with pleasure and his eyes alight, he smiled and asked, "Are you a ballerina?"

What if when Death comes to call, it takes the form of someone you are happy to see like that? Just like that.

A lifetime later, I find myself alone on 48th Street after a matinee. I walk to 8th Avenue and look for the tall window where I had written my name. The narrow little buildings are dirty, deteriorated, and disreputable looking. Air-conditioners and metal bars cover the windows. All changed and unrecognizable. I stand on the corner looking up. Where are they now, those excited, laughing girls with budding bodies in leotard, tights, and ballet slippers? Do I hear music from the second act of Swan Lake, drifting in the air?

Epilogue
The Hole in the Chainlink Fence
by Ruth Schaffer

Naomi cannot help but borrow sorrow.
She relates to another's pain, a rare quality
empathic to a point of despair.
She runs her hands through a forest of thick gray hair,
as if a good hair-pull will help her understand.

Persistent memory overtakes, overwhelms her
in mystery, which echoes after 50 years so scary
as to shiver her silver-ringed fingers, quiver
her lips in a half cry, half smile.

She admits it isn't fear of audience. As a teacher
she's faced many faces, many times. No,
it's the memory of the hole in the chainlink fence, with room
for only one to enter crawling.

The child is frightened, lost and alone.
Where is her sometimes Mother, the other kids,
the wooden tracks going nowhere? She is desperate
for home. Naomi's teary amber eyes meet yours,
plead "Why?" You are taken into her terror, unable
to help. You've been there as well, but in a
different dream, darker place, almost as bleak,
that only you may reveal in time.

November 17, 2013

Acknowledgments

My heartfelt gratitude to
Fred Hornbruch of Phileas Fogg Ventures
and
Sharon Wahl, The Fluent Scribe

www.ingramcontent.com/pod-product-compliance
Lightning Source LLC
Chambersburg PA
CBHW070629050426
42450CB00011B/3146